G1

Rosa Parks

by Michelle Levine

Compass Point Early Biographies

Content Adviser: Roger E. Bilstein, Ph.D., Professor of History Emeritus,
University of Houston-Clear Lake, Houston, Texas

Reading Adviser: Susan Kesselring, M.A., Literacy Educator,
Rosemount-Apple Valley-Eagan (Minnesota) School District

COMPASS POINT BOOKS
MINNEAPOLIS, MINNESOTA

Compass Point Books
3109 West 50th Street, #115
Minneapolis, MN 55410

Visit Compass Point Books on the Internet at *www.compasspointbooks.com*
or e-mail your request to *custserv@compasspointbooks.com*

Photographs ©: Taro Yamasaki/Time Life Pictures/Getty Images, cover, 25; Library of Congress, cover
background; Paul Schutzer/Time Life Pictures/Getty Images, 4; Hulton/Archive by Getty Images, 5, 14;
Bettmann/Corbis, 7, 18, 26; XNR Productions, 8; Corbis, 10; Robert W. Kelley/Time Life Pictures/Getty
Images, 11; Alabama Department of Archives and History, Montgomery, Alabama, 13, 21; Tony
Vaccaro/Getty Images, 16; AP/Wide World Photos/Pool, 17; Don Cravens/Time Life Pictures/Getty
Images, 20, 22, 23; Bill Pugliano/Getty Images, 24; AP/Wide World Photos/Dave Martin, 27.

Creative Director: Terri Foley
Managing Editor: Catherine Neitge
Editor: Brenda Haugen
Photo Researcher: Svetlana Zhurkina
Designer/Page production: Bradfordesign, Inc./Jaime Martens
Educational Consultant: Diane Smolinski

Library of Congress Cataloging-in-Publication Data
Levine, Michelle.
Rosa Parks / by Michelle Levine.
p. cm. — (Compass Point early biographies)
Includes bibliographical references and index.
ISBN 0-7565-0792-8 (hardcover)
1. Parks, Rosa, 1913—Juvenile literature. 2. African American women—Alabama—Montgomery—
Biography—Juvenile literature. 3. African Americans—Alabama—Montgomery—Biography—Juvenile
literature. 4. Civil rights workers—Alabama—Montgomery—Biography—Juvenile literature.
5. African Americans—Civil rights—Alabama—Montgomery—History—20th century—
Juvenile literature. 6. Segregation in transportation—Alabama—Montgomery—History—20th
century—Juvenile literature. 7. Montgomery (Ala.)—Race relations—Juvenile literature.
8. Montgomery (Ala.)—Biography—Juvenile literature. I. Title. II. Series.
F334.M753P38553 2005
323'.092—dc22   2004005690

Table of Contents

NOTE: In this book, words that are defined in the glossary
are in **bold** the first time they appear in the text.

Wanting Americans to Change

Rosa Parks believes all people are equal. White and black Americans were not treated the same when Rosa was growing up, though. Black people had to

Segregated shopping in the Southern states in the 1920s

follow unfair laws. Rosa wanted to change those laws and make life better for black people. One winter day in 1955, she did something very brave that made history.

This is Rosa's story.

◄ Rosa Parks in 1957

Born into an Unfair World

Life in Alabama in 1913 was much different than it is today. **Segregation** laws said black people and white people had to go to different schools. Black people could not drink from the same water fountains or go to many of the churches that white people could. Black people and white people did not live in the same parts of town.

Rosa was born into that world on February 4, 1913, in Tuskegee, Alabama. Her parents were James and Leona McCauley. James was a carpenter. Leona was a teacher.

FOR
COLORED
ONLY

Men drink from segregated water fountains.

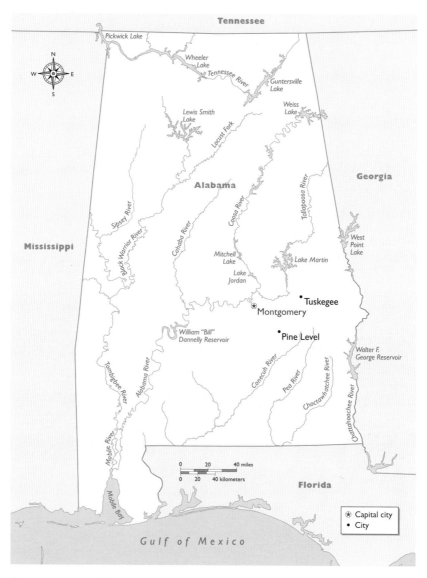

Rosa grew up in Alabama. She lived in Pine Level,
Montgomery, and Tuskegee.

When Rosa was 2, she moved to a small town near Montgomery, Alabama. The town was called Pine Level. She lived in Pine Level with her grandparents, her mother, and her younger brother, Sylvester.

Rosa's grandparents had been slaves. They told Rosa and Sylvester sad stories about how their lives were before they were free.

Rosa's grandparents also taught her and her brother they should be proud of who they were.

Segregation

Alabama was one of many Southern states that had segregation laws. These laws kept black people and white people apart.

White children ride a school bus as the black children walk to classes in 1954.

Many white people in Alabama did not treat black people with respect. They said black people were not equal to white people. Rosa knew better. She was as good as anyone else.

◄ Children in a segregated classroom in Tuskegee, Alabama, learn about corn and cotton in the early 1900s.

Rosa walked to the school for black children every day. All the black students in town shared one small classroom and one teacher. The white children went to a big school with many teachers. They also had a bus to drive them there. The black children had no bus.

When Rosa was 11 years old, she moved to Montgomery, Alabama, and lived with her aunt. Rosa went to a private school called the Montgomery Industrial School for Negro Girls. Rosa's mother did not have enough money to pay for Rosa to go to the school. Rosa helped clean classrooms so she could attend the school.

The streets of Montgomery in 1930

Fighting Segregation

In Montgomery, Rosa had to follow many segregation laws. She could not eat in most restaurants. She could not use the same

bathrooms that white people used. These laws made Rosa mad.

Rosa and other black people wanted to change the unfair laws. It was dangerous to speak out, however. Many black people were punished or harmed if they stood up for themselves.

When Rosa was 19, she married a man named Raymond Parks. Raymond risked his life to help other black people fight segregation. Rosa began to help black people, too.

◄ A restaurant sign says only white people are allowed in the dining room in 1955.

Rosa Takes Action

One law Rosa thought was unfair was about riding a city bus. This law said black people had to sit at the back of the bus. A black person also had to give up a seat if a white person wanted it.

Rosa sits in a 1950s era bus in Montgomery in 1995.

On December 1, 1955, Rosa took the
city bus home. She paid for her ride and found
a seat. Soon the bus filled up with people.

◄ In 1955, signs told black people they were
supposed to sit in the back of city buses.

17

Rosa's attorney, Charles D. Langford (right), walks with her as she goes to jail for the second time. Rosa was charged with violating segregation laws that brought about the bus boycott.

The bus driver told Rosa to give up her seat to a white man.

Rosa did something very brave. She said, "No." She was tired of being treated unfairly.

The bus driver threatened to have her arrested, but Rosa stayed in her seat. The police took Rosa to jail. She stayed there until her husband and some friends came to get her out.

The Bus Boycott

Rosa was angry. Other black people in Montgomery were angry, too. They were tired of following the unfair bus law.

The black people of Montgomery wanted to be brave like Rosa Parks. Four days after Rosa was arrested, black people in the

Remember we are Fighting For a cause Do Not Ride A Bus Today

NEGRO BOYCOTT POSTER

This is one of the posters which city policemen yesterday removed from bus stop posts as Negroes staged a boycott against the Montgomery City Lines over arrest of a Negro woman on a transportation segregation charge. The poster states: "Remember we are fighting for a cause. Do not ride a bus today."

Several thousand Negroes use the buses on a normal day.

Police cars and motorcycles followed the buses periodically to prevent trouble after Sellers said some Negroes reported they were threatened with violence if they rode buses yesterday.

The circulars distributed in Negro residential districts Saturday urging the boycott yesterday in protest to the arrest of Rosa Parks were not signed. The Rev. A. W. Wilson, pastor of the Negro church where the meeting was to be held, said he would not disclose "under any circumstances" the names of those who asked permission to use the church for the meeting.

Ministers of various churches led the meeting last night.

Earlier, Bagley had issued a statement saying the bus company "is sorry if anyone expects us to be exempt from any state or city law."

In the Rosa Parks case yesterday, the city was prepared to offer testimony from 11 witnesses. Only three, Blake and two women passengers testified. One of the women said there was an empty seat where Rosa Parks could have sat if she had moved to the rear.

As the boycott started yesterday morning, Negroes stood on downtown street corners waiting for rides or piled into taxicabs. Many walked two or three miles to work in the crisp cold weather.

Most Negro children walked to school and there was a relay auto pickup system operating throughout most of the day.

A boycott poster is printed in a Montgomery newspaper.

◄ The Reverend Martin Luther King Jr. talks about the bus boycott. Rosa sits in the front.

People carpool during the boycott as a bus sits empty across the street.

city decided to **boycott** the buses. They would stop riding them until the law changed. Martin Luther King Jr. helped lead the bus boycott. He was a Baptist minister in Montgomery.

The bus boycott lasted for more than a year. Black people walked to work or shared rides. The bus company lost a lot of money.

Rosa rides a bus following ➤
the end of the boycott.

Some white people wanted to stop the boycott. They didn't like black people standing up for themselves. They tried to scare Rosa and other black leaders, but the boycott went on. Finally, in 1956 the law was changed by the U.S. **Supreme Court.** The day after this happened, Rosa got on a bus and could sit anywhere she wanted.

An American Hero

Rosa was a hero. Americans all across the country heard about Rosa Parks and the bus boycott.

Not everyone liked what Rosa had done,

Rosa speaks to a group of young adults in November 1995.

though. Some people threatened Rosa and her family. She also lost her job as a **seamstress** because of the boycott. Rosa and Raymond decided to move to Detroit,

◀ The bus in which Rosa refused to give up her seat is on display in Dearborn, Michigan.

Civil rights marchers arrive at the Alabama Capitol to protest on March 30, 1965.

Michigan, in 1957 to be closer to her brother.

Rosa kept speaking out to Americans. She

told them that more laws had to change. She

said that black people and white people should be treated equally in all ways. Rosa's actions helped start the **civil rights movement.**

Today, Rosa is still a hero. She reminds people everywhere to stand up for fairness.

The street running by the Montgomery, Alabama, apartment where Rosa once lived is now named after her.

Important Dates in Rosa Parks's Life

1913	Born Rosa McCauley on February 4 in Tuskegee, Alabama
1924	Began going to a black girls' school in Montgomery, Alabama
1932	Married Raymond Parks on December 18
1943	Joined the National Association for the Advancement of Colored People (NAACP) to help make life better for black people
1955	Was arrested for not giving up her seat on a bus to a white man on December 1; took part in the Montgomery bus boycott
1956	The bus boycott ended on December 21 after the U.S. Supreme Court ruled that black people and white people have the same rights on buses
1957	Moved to Detroit, Michigan, with her husband and mother; began giving speeches to people all across the country about equality
1987	Opened the Rosa and Raymond Parks Institute for Self-Development in Detroit to help children of color
2003	Celebrated her 90th birthday at the Detroit Opera House

Glossary

boycott—to refuse to buy something or use a service as a form of protest

civil rights movement—in the 1950s and 1960s, an effort to gain black people equal treatment in the United States

seamstress—a woman whose job is sewing

segregation—a law or practice of keeping people or groups apart; segregation laws were used to keep black people and white people apart

Supreme Court—the most powerful court in the United States

Did You Know?

- Rosa learned how to read when she was 3 or 4 years old.

- In Montgomery, Rosa made a living as a seamstress, but her most important work was as secretary for the National Association for the Advancement of Colored People (NAACP).

- During the bus boycott, Rosa became good friends with Dr. Martin Luther King Jr. He went on to become a powerful leader in the struggle for equal rights during the 1950s and 1960s.

- Several streets have been named after Rosa, including Rosa L. Parks Avenue in Montgomery, Alabama. Rosa also has received many other honors and awards. They include the Congressional Gold Medal in 1999, the Lifetime Achievement Award in 1997, the Medal of Freedom in 1996, and the Martin Luther King Jr. Nonviolent Prize in 1980.

Want to Know More?

At the Library

Adler, David A. *A Picture Book of Rosa Parks.* New York: Holiday House, 1993.

Dubois, Muriel L. *Rosa Parks.* Mankato, Minn.: Bridgestone Books, 2003.

Parks, Rosa. *Dear Mrs. Parks: A Dialogue with Today's Youth.* New York: Lee & Low Books, 1996.

On the Web

For more information on *Rosa Parks,* use FactHound
to track down Web sites related to this book.

1. Go to *www.facthound.com*
2. Type in a search word related to this book
   or this book ID: 0756507928.
3. Click on the *Fetch It* button.

Your trusty FactHound will fetch the best Web sites for you!

On the Road

Rosa Parks Library and Museum
Troy State University Montgomery
251 Montgomery St.
Montgomery, AL 36104
334/241-8615
To learn about Rosa Parks, watch a re-enactment of the day Rosa was
arrested, learn about the bus boycott, and sit in the back row of a city bus

Index

About the Author
Michelle Levine is a children's book author and editor living in St. Paul, Minnesota.
She has worked in the field of children's nonfiction for the last six years.